I0794257

Sam and Pam

by Giulia Verzariu
illustrated by Rusty Fletcher

Decodable 1

McGraw Hill Education

Bothell, WA • Chicago, IL • Columbus, OH • New York, NY

MHEonline.com

Send all inquiries to:
McGraw-Hill Education
8787 Orion Place
Columbus, OH 43240

ISBN: 978-0-02-132283-1
MHID: 0-02-132283-X

Printed in the United States of America.

7 8 9 LCR 25 24 23

I am Sam.

I am sad.

I am Pam.

I am sad.

I see Sam!

I see Pam!